BRIMMING

Donna Langevin

PIQUANT PRESS

Copyright © Donna Langevin, 2019

ALL RIGHTS RESERVED. No part of this publication may be reproduced, stored in a retrieval system, or transmitted in any form or by any process – electronic, mechanical, photocopying, recording, or otherwise – without the prior written permission of the copyright owners and Piquant Press. The scanning, uploading and distribution of this via the internet or any other means without the permission of the publisher is illegal and punishable by law. Please purchase only authorized electronic editions, and do not participate in or encourage electronic piracy of copyrighted materials. Your support of the author's rights is appreciated.

Interior design and layout: James Dewar
Cover design: Susan Lynn Reynolds

Cover photo courtesy of BigStockPhoto.com
Photographer: Alex1975K

Published by Piquant Press,
13240 Mast Rd.,
Port Perry,
Ontario, Canada L9L 1B5.
www.piquantpress.ca

ISBN: 978-1-927396-15-5 (softcover)
ISBN: 978-1-927396-16-2 (e-book)

Printed and bound in Canada

1 2 3 4 5 6 7 8 9 10

for my brother, Gary
for my beloved sons, André, René and James

TABLE OF CONTENTS

IN LIEU OF AN ODE

In Lieu of an Ode	1
Visitation	5
Fences	6
Prayer to Saint Christopher	7
Bringing Back Mother	8
Candles for Gary	10
Le Calvaire d'Huberdeau	12
Advent, 1955	14
Benediction	16
Cinders	18
The Electric Ladies	20
Dispensation	22
Quebec Farm	24
Then and Now	25
The Blue Sleigh	26

TO STAY AFLOAT

Daring Niagara	31
The Orange Revenge	34
The Hand	36
Watching a Film Clip	38
Fulfillment	40
Keeping Your Word	42
Lady Niagara Falls	44
So When Are You Going Over Niagara Falls?	46

THE MAN WHO SLEPT BESIDE TORPEDOES

Biopsy	51
Side Effects	52
The Man Who Slept Beside Torpedoes	53
Tumour Talk	55
Nocturne	56
White	57
Submarine Fare	58
When the Door Opened	59
Frustration	60
Hallelujah!	61
The Sound of Survival	62

THE THING IN THE MIRROR

After a Fall on the Sidewalk	65
Relive	66
Waves	67
Comfort	68
Missing	69
Mad Hatter	70
Post-op Driving Home	71
After the Accident	72
Grounded	73
Gardener	74
Hear	75
The Unveiling of the New Nose	76

TESTS OF THE HEART

Family Tree	79
4 a.m.	80
Vigil	81
René	82
Looking at Old Postcards	83

Growing Up	84
What hurts most	85
Standing Guard	86
Ode to an IV Tree	88
Because	89
Umbilical	90
Tips	91
Angels	92
Helium	93
Tests of the Heart	94
Thanksgiving	96

THE STORIES THAT WRITE US

DNA	99
Sapphira's Story	100
Dinah Nuthead	102
Origami	104
The Many Holes in a Snowflake	106
A year after your passing, mom	107
Sparrow	108
Brimming	110
An Old Yarn	111

End Notes	113
Acknowledgements	116
A Special Thanks To…	118
Author Bio	119

IN LIEU OF AN ODE

In Lieu of an Ode
for my brother, Gary

You were dusting our parents' names,
I was trimming peonies,
the long grass roping our ankles
in Notre-Dame-des-Neiges cemetery.

Later, our nephew posted on Facebook
Nana and Grampa are looking real good
and I think, yeah six feet under,
then I realize he means you and me, Gary.

What if I write
your heart was recently bridged
by leg-veins the color
of the frozen stream that circles
your home in the mountains
where the ghost of a former owner
who hanged himself from a rafter
roams into the bedrooms.

What if I write I waited
for forty years of snow
to melt, our parents to take off
to the underworld
and our children to become human
before I understood
that you are no longer the brat
who snipped off
my doll's eyelashes,
bloodied our brother Greg's head
with a toy rake.

You've outgrown
the teen who poured
an eel down my neck,
hid shackled nudes
in porn mags under your bed
and teased, *Your teeth are like stars—*
they come out at night.
Your hair is like wheat—
yellow and stringy.
I am no longer the *wounded Wilma*
our mother called *the whiney*
with a lump in her throat
or the saintly sister who prayed
in a convent high-school
for you to perish.

What if I write
now that you're seventy
you nickname me "coffin bait"
and feed your dog at the table
with a shared fork
(yes, salad with croutons and raisins,
vegan curry with mangoes)
in hopes he'll guide you
through Hades.

And what if I add
you are also the angel
who called every day to ask
how I was when mother was dying.
The one who devoured
every word in my books and informed

Greg, now a lawyer,
that I'd be famous after my death
while he'd be toast forever.

You are the bro with a booklist
as long as the path 'round your lake
who showed me the way
to Wharton and Kate Chopin
and hounded me to write
an Ozymandias-sonnet
or an ode for you like an obit
you could savour alive.

And to my surprise you are
the only child of five
who loves our parents enough
to share the same worms and dirt,
snuggle right up to their bones
like when you were a kid
jumping into bed with them.

And to my constellation-sized wonder
I discover I love you enough
to lie here beside you
(yes, for eternity)
though I've drawn up my will to escape
to a Scotch Pine by Georgian Bay
with my dog's ashes for company.

And what if I write
Gary, you don't fit into an ode.
Your life doesn't rhyme.

Your rhythm ran off on binges
before you embraced AA and became
a seven-star father and grandpa.
Yes, I'd need an epic or saga.

So, would you be satisfied
if I write I want to return often
to hike your Laurentian lake and explore
the rosary of tiny French towns
named after saints?
That I want to brave
the ghost in your house,
feed your mutt
with my own fork
before the long grass
and peonies in Notre-Dame
flourish in your ashes
or my Scotch Pine claims me first.

Visitation

Twenty years ago Guy was still half a kid,
when it happened, my brother said,
mid-thirties, like our own sons are now.
His sister never went upstairs again
and forbade her child
to set foot on the steps.

In my brother's house
the ghost of the former owner
still swings
from a rafter near my bed.

The wind dirges and frets.
The feet of a pale shadow
dance along my blinds.
I toss and turn, raging
at the wraith who will haunt
his family forever, who stirs
my fear for my own sons.

When nightmares chased them,
they'd leap into bed with me,
snuggle up to my spine,
hide their faces in my hair.

The mother in me awakes to untie
this poor blue man,
let him down into my arms.

Fences

How do you fence a ghost?
Nothing to shred
on barbed wire, nothing
to snag his soul.
A barn-owl could devour him
and stay hungry.

How do you draw property lines
he won't laugh at and leap over?

Should you ask for his passport
as if he were a refugee
at the border of your garden
or try to capture
his fingerless prints?

Perhaps you keep him out
by letting him in,
setting a place at your table,
an extra chair by the fireplace.
Admit that the beam
where he hung himself
also holds up your house.

Prayer to Saint Christopher

O Patron Saint of Travelers
bless my brother's veins.

Protect their miles of waterways
and tributaries that feed

the islands of his organs.
May their blood sing clearly,

glow like ripe strawberries and bypass
the clots of Camembert and bacon fat.

Bless the microbe fish that swim through
their skeins. Please render them harmless.

Let their salt be sea-worthy,
their pulse, strong as eels.

Beloved Saint, safeguard
the veins that map him.

May they never bleed
except to save his life.

May they lay down
their lengths like soldiers

to be sewn into bridges
in the battle for his heart.

Bringing Back Mother

Driving to Mont-Tremblant
Gary and I dare
Laurentian back roads
up
     and
           around hairpins,
past crosses with plastic flowers
we climb
         into the last century
of fieldstone farmhouses
barns faded like old straw,
cottages perched
         so close to the river
you could fish from the windows.

My brother gets sky-high on sugar
as his bag of peppermints shrinks.
Steps on the gas, cracks open
the back window and riles
his German Shepherd.

Now for some entertainment, Duke!
Bark hello to the cows.
Make 'em budge off their butts
and give 'em horses a run.
Hey Duke look at that graveyard,
the folks who lived in the farmhouse
have their own private plot.
C'mon Duke. Bark your brains out.
Wake up the dead!

Mont-Tremblant, blasted
by snow-guns that shroud
the black-diamond ski runs
trembles in the distance.
Gary recalls our mother
buried on Mount Royal last year.

I wish I could tell mom I'm sorry
when I never wanted to visit.
I hated her growing old, scared
of becoming like her.
Now she's in my arthritic bones
and I wear her wrinkly skin
but she's not here to comfort me.

Candles for Gary

I choose this stone-faced church
because you love dogs
and in *St. Paul's* park
a Red Setter runs free.

Inside the nave, the saint
on the ceiling points
to a gold-lettered sign,
Saule, Quid me persequeris*
The verb sounds like perspire.
I want to get the hell out
but have a promise to keep—

There was blood soaking
my socks and hospital gown
My hands dripped
like an axe murderer's,
you pleaded on the phone
after the stent ruptured.
Look Sis, I know you're an ex-Catholic,
but please find a church,
light a candle and pray
that Québec's lousy health-care system
schedules my bypass damn soon.

I light a wine-coloured vigil lamp
in front of plaster Jesus,
his Sacred Heart leaking
ruby drops. Skirting
the stained-glass Last Supper

I bite back the thought:
If the Good Shepherd dines on roast lamb,
and I'm the family black sheep
why should He listen to me?

When it comes to answering prayers,
my grade-school teacher, Sister Celine claimed
the Virgin Mary is softer than God
so I kneel in her alcove, fire up
a row of candles that smell
like burnt marshmallows,
the bonfires you love,
and the hearth in your home.

Le Calvaire d'Huberdeau
founded in 1891 by the Fathers of Montfort, Quebec

A golden Christ on a huge
wooden cross looms
over the corn and cabbage fields.
Blood trickles down the mountain
mingling with that of the animals
slaughtered on the farms
while the tears of the two Marys
who weep at his nailed feet
flood La Rivière-Rouge.

When I tell my brother
this shrine, flanked
by the Stations of the Cross,
weighs on my spirits and blights
the view from the valley, I wonder
how people housed in its shadow
can laugh, dance or make love.

***

When Christ came loose
from his crumbling pine cross
as it sank into the soil, I wish
the priests and parishioners had laid
him down in the sweet spring grass,
farmers' wives had spooned broth into him—
then, while he slept they'd plucked
thorns from his brow, anointed
his wounds with Bee Balm,

dressed him in clean
overalls and a flannel shirt
and carried him to a farmhouse
to rest in a sleigh-bed
until he grew strong enough
to sit in a rocking chair
and cluck at the hens or pick
berries purpling the garden.

O how I wish
that instead of welding him
to a longer-stronger cast-iron cross,
the people had loved Christ enough
to play cards and drink *Caribou* with him
as he warmed himself by the fireside
under the wings
of their snow-feathered roofs.

Advent, 1955

Sister Celine, my grade-four teacher
calls us her daughters.
She hands us mimeographs of the stoles,
maniples and chasubles
priests wear at mass.
We crayon them in liturgical colours—
violet, white, red, green and gold
while she trains the altar boys
to swing frankincense,
tinkle the Sanctus bells,
shape their lips around Latin
and hold the paten under
the chins of communicants
who tongue up the wafers

the kitchen nuns
roll, slice and bake in a woodstove
that wilts their wimples,
and smoke-stains their skins,
while their sisters,
the laundry-nuns, sweating
in coarse woolen habits
hand-wash, starch and iron
the lace-trimmed surplices
sewn by the ones threading
their paths to the Lord
one stitch at a time as they pray
with pins in their mouths.

***

To secure a spot in heaven
a Québecois farmer gives away
his tenth child to the church
for a small dowry.
Sister Celine, now middle-aged,
once dreamt of bearing a child.

Her expectations during Advent
about to be fulfilled,
she unlocks a cabinet,
takes out the crèche,
joins the stable-joints,
buffs the tarnished star,
grooms the plaster donkey
and places it near the manger
filled with immaculate straw.

She rounds up the sheep
stored in egg-cartons
to graze on green cloth pastures.
Dusting Mary, Joseph
and the three Kings,
she stations the figurines.

Labouring to free the child
swaddled in last year's newsprint
held in a paper bag 'womb'
she cuts the purple cord,
cradles Him in her palms,
his head, shoulders, body
delivered into the world.

Benediction

Once a country retreat
owned by Jesuit priests,
a blessing to brighten
my brother's house
with its dark cell-sized bedrooms
and the same narrow planks
that walled confessionals
where I knelt and whispered
my childhood sins.

A prayer to soften
the pine knot eyes reproaching
my lover and me
as they once spied on
priests who scourged their souls
after entering
each other,
then chanted their way
up the dirt road
to the neighboring home,
run by the Good Shepherd nuns,
to dole out communion
to girls without rings
who laundered, scrubbed
and gave birth to orphans.

A supplication for stains
on the floorboards
here in my brother's abode,
today's waking sun tints

the tones of warm maple syrup
as my lover laughs and licks me.

A blessing on the tarred beams
sawed from century-old oaks
that bear up
our bedroom ceiling.

A benediction
for shuttered windows
we throw open to let in
the hymn of the wind caressing
treetops and ferns,
the songs of mating birds
that brush the roof
with the sacred shadows
of wings.

Cinders

Built in the 1850's
by Irish and Scottish settlers
in the township of Shrewsbury,
a small Anglican church watched over
its loved ones asleep
in the cemetery ringed
by dark forest spires.

A century later, the bells
were thrice stolen, the base
of the steeple kicked in.
The sacred dwelling—
axed, hammered
and spray painted.

In 2014, a hellish fire melted
history and fed
on the ancestral church
turning its bones to cinders
sprinkled by snow.

Today, treading softly
between toppled tombstones
soot-blackened or defaced,
my Irish brother and I wonder
(like so many others leafed from
Papist and Protestant trees)
if this was the deed of teen arsonists
fueled by drugs or booze?

Or perhaps a heated descendant, inspired
by a ghost walk or séance,
tried to enflame
the spirits of Orangemen
who rooted themselves
in the richest farmland and fenced out
the French faith and tongue.

Whoever's conscience may
still reek of smoke,
my brother and I pick our way
through the plots, breathe
a prayer for the dead,
trying not to crush
the bluebells
and tiny buttercup chalices
springing from the graves.

The Electric Ladies

Miles of transmission towers
        stretch
                above the treetops
between St. Cesaire and Tracy.

At eighteen, my brother got a summer job
painting those ladies
red, yellow or checkerboard
to warn planes away.

Agile as an ape, he'd climb
up a steel skeleton
toward the skein of wires
where a slipup
could fry his flesh.

Wanting to get in good
with the crew who applauded
his "acrobat act" after he hooked
on his safety belt wrong,
    slipped
        and flipped
   upside-down
attached
        to a suspension wire,
he volunteered
to watch from a "safe perch"
and wave his paintbrush to warn

his mates in the field to hide
their brown-bagged bottles
from the boss dusting the dirt road
in his horse and buggy.

Mid-summer, when Gary told mom
those dames stored
enough juice in their *pots*
to power the electric chair
and barbecue Quebec,
her hair bristled,
her steely eyes flashed,
she begged and offered
sky-high bribes
      if only,
           if only he'd quit.

But Gary was wed to those ladies,
and by god, he was no *damn chicken*
even after his friend forgot
to wear rubber-soled shoes
and fell and broke his back.

Wow Gary, that story's electric! I shout
fifty years later, as we drive past
his towering wives.

His hands glow on the steering wheel,
his grin lights up the landscape.

Dispensation

Thou shalt not eat
anything with a face or a mother,
my brother's heart-smart bible commands.
Thou shalt not be tempted
by eggs, cheese or bacon.
Beans and veggies are kosher.

A year after his triple bypass,
Gary, who used to wolf down
meat 'by the herd'
is now lean as a string-bean.

What keeps him faithful?

Once a month, on a Friday,
he treats himself to a meal
he rules his 'papal indulgence
during his perpetual Lent.'

Instead of choking down naked tofu,
an unbuttered baked potato
or salt-free lentils and rice,
he heads for a French town—
St-Pierre, St-Simon, or St-Thomas—
apostles of deep-fried fish
and patron saints of Poutine.

He orders haddock 'baptized in oil'
and king-size fries with gravy.
Savouring his forbidden feast,
he forks up the last mouthful, wipes
grease from his grin
and dons his halo again.

Quebec Farm
after a painting by Anne Savage, 1935

Sunlight blesses the clouds.

A road, narrow
     as a priest's purple stole
leads beyond
    the tilting
        fence posts
from house to
           neighbourly farmhouse
on the green mountain that mothers
     an old woman bent for tending
   her late-blooming garden
on the meadow's golden hem.

I'm tempted to linger
but her angular house
     and the weathervane rooster's claws
caution me
   soon the north wind will hone
the fold of her peaked slate roof.

The mountain will don
     a white-wimple,
the snowbound valley
cloistering me until spring.

Then and Now

In the hell-raising days
when your coal eyes
flashed lightning,
you sported
a puck-blackened front tooth,
you and your buddies would shoot
the white-clawed jagged rapids
on *La Grande Rivière.*

Sweating under wood-ribbed canoes,
you'd curse mosquitoes à la couriers-des-bois,
swig Sortilège by the campfire, skewer
the cook for *burned dog food*
and tell the tale of the devil's flying canoe
that shadowed a steeple
and crashed.

Those escapades vanished with wood smoke
and later, the ghosts of your friends;
today you feed bread to the fish in your lake
as dragonflies dance past your rowboat,
flat-bottomed as a frying pan.

Tomato sauce tins for bailers
and a long natal rope,
you chant the rhyme our grandmother sang
swinging your arms in the nursery.

Dipping your oars in the sunset now,
you teach your grandkids to row.

The Blue Sleigh

after a painting by Sarah Robertson, Québec 1924

Forget your new Nissan
buried like a loaf of grey bread
in your snow-crusted driveway.

Imagine instead, Gary,
a white horse with black blinkers
like the milkman's horse of our childhood
that lipped sugar lumps from our palms.
See, he is yoked to the blue sleigh waiting
outside your Laurentian log home
built on the mountain-side
more than a century ago.

The horse's flanks are steaming,
icicles drip from his chin,
his breath ghosts the air
as he paws the drifts.

Imagine also the two bent figures
taking their seats in the sleigh
with rounded backs turned to the world
are you and I, in dark
woolen capes and swaddled
in fur blankets.

Though you grasp the reins
it is the horse who will guide us
past faded barns,
farmhouses with lace-shrouded windows,
across a melting bridge
into green meadows where
we'll sleep like snuggled-up children.

TO STAY AFLOAT

Daring Niagara
for Annie Edson Taylor, 1901*

Ride the Falls in a barrel?
Listen to me, McWhisker.
When I imagine Horseshoe Falls
bucking me over the drop
my stomach churns white water.

Brave the Falls alone?
I might as well ride in a casket.
Besides, I'm no daredevil, McWhisker.
Sensible shoes, high-necked
dress buttoned to my chin.
At age 62, I secure
the feather to my hat
with safety pins,
carry an umbrella for balance.

O please stop meowing, McWhisker.
These last three sardines are mine.
You wolfed down your share this morning.
You know the rules.
One can a day between us.

No, I don't want to dance
in the mist with the Reaper
though I once spun
in a ballroom studio in Michigan.

No, I don't want to drown
like a pickle in brine.

May my last breath be scented
with juniper and sage
from the mountains peering down
on Mexico City where I couldn't find a job.

No, you can't have more milk, puss.
One pint a week between us.
These last drops— for my tea.
But ... if you and I ...
ah ... if we were a team at the Falls ...
imagine if we got lucky!

Instead of scraping by
à la Old Mother Hubbard, we'd feast
on steak and roast-beef with gravy.
I'd buy a house with a library.
You could purr on the windowsill
lapping up creamy sunshine.

Don't hiss at me, McWhisker
and stiffen your fur to needles.
Can't you see us now?
A barrel padded with my mattress. Our lucky
heart-shaped pillow under my head,
you in my arms ...
Heroine Annie Edson Taylor
and brave McWhisker, her CAT
That's what I'd paint on the barrel!

Quit clawing my chest, McWhisker.
A foolproof oak and iron-ribbed barrel ...
We'll test it first
to see if it leaks.
Dare to live your dreams, I chalked
on the board for my students to copy
on slates at Sault Ste. Marie.

Long before your eyes widened, Puss,
my husband fell in the war. I struggled
since then to win my bread,
but a woman earns
pennies compared to a man
and the last of our dreams
will soon wash away
when I can't afford
this damp dingy room
and daily sardines to survive.

To stay afloat and ... Yes,
we need a grand plan ...
The Pan-Am is coming to Buffalo,
we could draw a rich crowd.
At the very least, we'll become a legend
bigger than Puss n' Boots.

Think of it this way, McWhisker,
cats have nine lives.
The odds are in our favour.

The Orange Revenge
*for Bobby Leach, July 25, 1911**

Barnum and Bailey stuntman,
owner of a restaurant
on Bridge St., Niagara Falls,
you slurp an orange
and brag to your customers
your plans to eclipse
Annie Taylor's success

*Anything she can do, I can do better**
Your barrel gets stuck
near Devil's Hole whirlpool
and has to be hooked out

Yes, anything Annie can do ...
After her lucky ride
Horseshoe Falls kicks you
into the hospital for months
with broken kneecaps and jaw

Later, parachuting
        into the river
from Upper Suspension Bridge
your silky, tentacled sky-fish
      floats you
   off course to Canada
dangerously close to the Falls

Yes, anything, anything ...
you keep crowing
as riches rain down on your tours
of the USA, England and Canada
where you preen and pose
with your barrel wowing
hobble-skirted women
with drooping plumed hats
at lectures and vaudeville shows
till Lady Luck leaves
an orange peel in your path

Your fall breaks your leg
which the surgeon hacks off
in an attempt to save you
from gangrene the colour
of envy.

The Hand
    for Charles G. Stephens, July 11, 1920*

I am the hand
on billboards, posters and websites
   reaching
      out of a barrel
         trapped
in sleeves of white water

I am the hand
at the end of the arm
still strapped inside the barrel,
the right hand that misses
its twin
and the head, torso and feet

the hand of the *Demon Barber from Bristol*
whose body the Falls ripped out,
now gristle in ghost stories

The harebrained hand that belonged
to a granite-willed stuntman
so determined to feed
his wife and brood of eleven
he refused advice
to test his unwieldy barrel,
carry enough oxygen
and free his feet
bound to an anvil for ballast

I am the hand wristed to the tattooed arm
Don't Forget Me Annie

The hand that fishes the sky
tears at white-bread-clouds
and plucks
at meaty ducks
near the base of the Falls

I am the golden hand that beckons
to billions of tourists

the drowning hand that will grasp you
and pull you under

the hand that never earned one penny
for the starving widow and children.

Watching a Film Clip
for George Stathakis, July 4, *1930*

With my first glimpse
I fall in love with you, George—
fine-featured Adonis
with thundercloud hair
and the body of Michelangelo's David
in a black silk suit.

My knuckles turn white as rapids
when your helpers lift
the lid of your jaunty
red, white and blue-striped barrel
and you whistle towards the opening,
climb into its womb,
your hand, a brave flower,
stems from the hole to wave.

Greek immigrant employed
as a chef in Buffalo,
you poached the sun
spilled constellations of salt grains
and conducted the music humming
from the lips of wineglasses
and pronged on the tines of forks.

Ready to gamble your life
for funds to print
your books on "being and knowing"
the Houses refused to publish
you bank instead
on romance, mystery and thrillers
and build your own barrel,
a ten-foot coffin.

Twenty-six hours later, Horseshoe Falls
disgorges your weight
trapped behind white curtains.

The mouth pried open
you are extracted,
blue as a stillborn,
but your ancient pet turtle
still strong as the tortoise that bears
the world on its shell
crawls out of your sleeve
on the legs of a new legend.

Fulfillment
for Nathan Boya, AKA, William Fitzgerald, July 15, 1961

Whoever you were
(or told the police you were
when they greeted you with handcuffs)
you rose through the hole
of your rubber ball
after Horseshoe Falls whipped off
the hatch

Whatever the motive
for your near fatal feat—

> a tribute to Kenyan nationalist leader
> Tom Mboya whose name you adopted
> in the police station,
> or the secret leaked out decades later
> on "To Tell the Truth"—
> to atone a jilted woman
> for a called-off engagement
> and honeymoon at Niagara

Whatever your revisions, you risked
disturbing the universe
and *squeezed it into a ball**
you dubbed the "Plunge-O-Sphere"
to grasp your own grandeur—
the first black man in history
to bounce like a *peach** over the Falls

Nearing the end
of my own career
of plunges into poetry
marriages, motherhood, teaching,
I do not measure
fulfillment *in teaspoons**
or the sum
of spectacular feats

> *I had to do this*
> *I wanted to do this*
> *and I am glad I did it,*

I hope to say, as you did at your trial,
when I face my last self-judgement.

Keeping Your Word
for Karel Soucek, July 2, 1984*

When my son promised the press
he'd conquer Horseshoe Falls in a barrel,
I steeled my spine
and reminded him
he'd have to deed his word
unlike those braggarts who palmed off
fictitious Falls plunges
at freak shows and lecture halls
where paupers paid hard-earned dimes.

I birthed
Karel's beautiful long-limbed body
finely wrought features
and perfect backbone.
Every sunrise he'd break
me open again as he stood
at the top of the Falls.

How could I let him risk
the bones I fed with fish soup,
dumplings and honey cake?

I punished his first fib
with a teaspoon of hot mustard
forced between clenched baby teeth.

It's not whether you triumph or fail,
it's that you keep your word...
or at least try!

Karel painted my words on his barrel
before he conquered the Falls.

I basked for a while in his glory
till fear clawed at me again—

to fund a museum to immortalize
his stunt, Karel climbed
to the neon stars
in Houston's Astrodome
to plunge in his barrel
from the 180 foot height
into a pool below.

On the night his ill-balanced barrel
perched at the end of the platform,
the restless crowd heckled
for its release; I held my breath
as he let fly the word that smashed
his skull like crockery on the rim of the tank.

Holding my son's limp body,
I'd give my life to have taught him
to love himself enough
to send down an empty barrel
on the wings of a life-saving lie.

Lady Niagara Falls
for Jesse W. Sharp, June 5, 1990

When it came to mastering
Lady Niagara,
you, a dashing young
stuntman par excellence
turned up your nose
at barrels with fat ageing bodies
wooden waists banded with steel
breath stinking of brine
and opted
for your reed-slender kayak
streamlined as a shark.

Without so much as a kiss, you planned
to cleave the Lady's skin with your paddle
spread her silky wet lips
ride on the back
of her breathtaking speed
and fly over the brink
above her raging waters
then land a gull in the rapids
without a single look back.

Oh, you were so sure of your plan
you refused to wear a helmet
so your triumphant face could be caught
on camera as you roller-coasted
the gorge four miles down her torso
into her "Pipeline" with jade-coloured swells

then skirted her Whirlpool heart
to land high and dry at Lewiston
where you'd booked a victory dinner!

But Lady Niagara, no lover
of bachelors who specialize
in quick conquests,
pummeled your plans to pieces
married your bones to her fury
and ate your remains
no one has ever found.

In the Lewiston restaurant,
candles remain unlit,
the plates go hungry—
the spirit of Lady Niagara
dines alone.

So when are you going over Niagara Falls in a barrel?

I already went over the brink
when I met you, darling.

I took a plunge
walking your dogs.
I twisted my spine
shredded my lips,
my broken nose flooding
the sidewalk.

I crashed too
through the watery curtain
of our candlelit shower
and my bruise aped Niagara's rainbow.
Not to mention
the hatch of my heart ripped off,
my ballast
        shifted
every time your wife called
and you purred into the phone.

In my nightmares
I melt into Lori Martin, who embraced
Horseshoe Falls with two-timer
daredevil Steve Trotter
in a barrel narrower than a single bed,
sharing her last sips of oxygen
while firefighters risked
their own lives
to rescue her from a romance

that would later fracture
her neck off Golden Gate Bridge
on a "Tarzan swing" with Stevie.
That stunt slammed him in jail and left her
pining on a hospital bed, while I

with not much left to break, dear,
am forced to question my longing.

THE MAN WHO SLEPT BESIDE TORPEDOES
poems for a submariner

Biopsy

Today you lie with pants half-mast
cheeks spread wide

The doctor inserts an ultrasound probe

A bawdy song you loved to sing on the submarine—

I put my hand upon her twat,
She said, "Hey Yankee, you're hittin' the spot ...

There are no words to cheer you now

A snap-gun zaps needles
through your wall into the prostate plum
and cores out samples of flesh

One needle ... two needles ... three ...
you count them down like underwater moments
until you reach twelve

Nerves strung tight as wires
dreading each shock, you pray
to the goddess, *Novocaine.*

Side Effects

I'm used to the sight of my own blood
Don't worry my love, I say
as cum makes poppies on the bed sheet

Tiny clotted robins nesting
in our pubic hair,
we wash each other in the shower
warm as April rain.

The Man Who Slept Beside Torpedoes

As a child, you never wanted
to be Huck Finn riding a river-raft
or to join Swiss Family Robinson
shipwrecked by a storm.

You preferred running barefoot
on your grandpa's farm,
your only ships—
                the woodchips
launched and raced on the river.

If the ship rocks don't board it— your motto
for boats and your life
until Uncle Sam forced you to choose
a foxhole in Vietnam,
or seasick duty on a Navy submarine.

Gliding under the sea's skin
in your rubber-coated cocoon—

who gives a rat's ass for storms on the surface
at a hundred and forty feet down
(though there's always the risk of a water-line leak
or a fatal brush with live wires)

You bunked beside the torpedoes.

At twenty-five, the Navy made you a link
in the long chain of command
to a nuclear missile launch.

Today, post Fukushima,
you don't go to sea.
You stick close to your onshore desk.
Your only missile—a vintage
torpedo-shaped pen for drafting
plans to safeguard us.

Tumour Talk

Today you dared to share
your news with the guys at the nuclear plant.

Surprise!
        A bunch of them
told tumour tales too.

—My tumour is bigger than yours.

—Well, mine's more dangerous.

—Hell, mine's the most expensive. Going to bankrupt
my goddamn insurance company.

—Mine wins the prize!
Shot full of radioactive isotopes,
the alarms here went ballistic.

—Shit, mine is smarter than yours.
It beat the technology!

Hey buddy, you're not alone.

Nocturne

What if that tumour slides to my balls,
tries for a home run?

What if it eats my bones and brain
so I never work again?

What if insurance turns me down
or the deductible's more than I earn?

What if,
    what if,
        what if...

You plead with the God you dumped,
cry for your long-dead mom.

In the morning, you dress in your daytime-self.
Piss on cancer! Fuck it!

You josh with the guys at work.
Put fear in your locker.

Until light in the dugout dwindles
into the lonely night.

White

During radiation, you must eat
white for weeks

White bread, white potatoes, white yogurt
plain chicken breast,
the pallid flesh of pears

Grains, seeds, nuts, peels, fat or fibre
dark vegetables—forbidden

The beam burns your tumour,
shrivels its fingers
Your nails blanch
Your olive skin turns pale

You become the man in the moon,
dark circled eyes
crescent mouth downcast

At the table together, I eat like a sparrow—

but while you wane and sink,
I sneak pocketed cashews,
wolf down dates and plums

You doze in front of TV,
a book sleeping on your chest

I exercise in sunlight
to gain strength to sustain you
with love in every colour.

Submarine Fare

What did you eat on the sub, I ask
as you push away your white
meal of mashed potatoes and yogurt.

Oh, the food was real decent down there—

Square eggs loaded with ketchup
Fried Gorilla steaks
Shit on a Shingle
and ice cream from a machine.

When the Door Opened …

the one you described
as made from steel and concrete
with no handles or knobs

impregnable as a bank vault
or gate to a medieval castle

a door stronger than the Great Wall of China,
the one built by Emperor Constantine,
seamless as a no-exit nightmare

After giant machines lasered
your tumor with light
and the door to the treatment room opened

the Crusader Castle crumbled

the bank vault sprung open

the Great Wall of China and the one around Byzantium
   came
       tumbling
             down

because I was there on the other side

      holding out my arms.

Frustration

When you were a child being potty-trained
you and your dad stood by the toilet
sinking paper boats with your streams of pee.

At twelve you sniggered when Gulliver
pissed on a fire in Lilliput,
and one drunken night by Lake Ponchartrain
you and your buddies gleefully
put out the campfire by whizzing full-blast.

Tonight, after the lasers
bombarded your tumour again,
you've gotten up for the fifth time.

You coax yourself with a running tap
the thought of a garden hose
and a photo of Niagara Falls.

But only a dribble leaks out.

Hallelujah!

Three months after treatment, you can
make love again, and so we do as if

we can make the sun rise
melt winter's white bodice

coax amarilla and sweetbush
from Sonora sand

O, we laugh in New York
Venice and Camelot

I stroke your magician's wand
You open the portal of paradise

You are my silky rabbit
I show you my basket of Easter Eggs

Hot from miracle-making,
we toss aside the bed sheets

The Sound of Survival

I love that you dare
>   to swim up
>   from your hospital trawler
>   nightmares
with hooks and nets.

You insist
>   on playing again
like the dolphins
in the wake
>   of your submarine
surfacing close to land.

Oh I love
>   your
>   leaping

>   flippant

resilient self

that risks a ride
on the white hats
>   and scarves
of laughter's waves.

THE THING IN THE MIRROR

After a Fall on the Sidewalk

Kermit the Frog lips

A boxer's side-swung nose

Purple-ringed raccoon eyes
        puzzling
the *thing* in the mirror.

        I waggle
my Chaplin moustache-stitches
tugging at my raw skin and wonder

Where is my face?

Relive

Walking the dog
Susie spots a rabbit
her leash yanks tight
i laugh *ya dumb mutt*
that's not a rabbit   it's all in your head
C'mon let's go to the beach
then i stumble against a ridge
launch into the air
   at the end
     of the leash
WHACK!
        my face slams into the sidewalk
bones crunch
blood spouts from my nose
runs down my throat
no this can't be me
it's all in my head
i am not spitting out mouthfuls
it's just my tripped
imagination vomiting
clots on the concrete.

Waves

roll toward me
the first red breakers of pain
crash over me on the sidewalk
the undertow drags me into the warmth
that sucks me down
and drowns Jim's voice
don't go to sleep
i sink into drowsy swells
no you can't go to sleep

concussion
        concussion
rhymes with percussion,
my head, a timpani
drummed by a mallet

wake up
      wake up
           wake up

i drift out further ebbing away

his voice tows me back.

Comfort

Jim can't kiss my inner tube lips
stroke my clown nose
or caress my squirrel cheeks

but he holds my hand and whispers
You are still lovely to me
recalling how
I wrapped my love around him
the summer his tumor grew

Both of us then and now
broken beautiful.

Missing

This twisted mess isn't my nose
It's an imposter
a stand-in

My real nose has gone AWOL

Is it sniffing a lilac bush
the scent of heady wine
or snorting
the steam on hot chocolate

Perhaps a blackbird snapped it up
to feed to its hatchlings

Maybe it's sunbathing on a beach,
inhaling the mould in the Sistine Chapel

or forsaking me, has attached itself
to a noseless Roman statue

I'll put up a poster—

MISSING NOSE:
Patrician, in its 7th decade
No freckles or sunspots

REWARD IF FOUND:
An all-expenses paid trip for two nostrils
to a parfumerie in Paris.

Mad Hatter

My nose is a bone china spout
on grandma's hand-painted teapot

The pot slips
    from a picnicker's hand
        shatters against a boulder
covered with watercress leaves

Blue windmills fly
    A shepherdess loses her sheep

A piccolo plays a lament
    as my broken nose pours
        red tea.

Post-op Drive Home

The apple trees open pink puffs
Plum trees shake out lace.

Turkey vultures blacken the branches—
also filled with grace.

The day steps out from a golden cloud
softer than a fawn.

When I set forth from the car
I am Jesus on Percodan
walking a sea-green lawn.

After the Accident

I am terrified
of tripping
on a dandelion
a worm
a bad luck crack
in a sidewalk

Petrified
of slipping
on a sunbeam
neon ray
dust moat
or sand-wrinkle

I wish for a world
with mountains and anthills
flattened into plains
a mood stable
as a nailed down plank
instead of this diving board.

Grounded

I no longer spiral with contrails
or coast with a V of geese
on an airy wing

Frightened of falling face down
I scrutinize the sidewalk
square
     by
timeworn square
    for cracks
       upheavals
          tilted manhole lids
banana peels and bones.

Gardener

My blood spattered the sidewalk,
floated off flakes of my flesh
sowed the earth

Could something take root from my face-plant?

    a tomato patch
      roster of radishes
bed of get-well roses
or a harvest of raspberry canes

I'm tending my wounds like a gardener
who mulches good soil.

I'm soothing
    my stitches with ointment
and guarding
    my splinted nose
from dogs and paws of children
in hopes I'll bloom as a sunflower.

Hear

the slippery
       g
        l
         i
          s
           s
            a
             n
              d
             o
of a woodwind phrase

a featherless robin
          f
         a
          l
           l
            i
             n
              g

a pebble
    tossed ....
                    into Basho's pond
the ashes

    ti
    pp
    ed

from Magritte's pipe.

Unveiling the New Nose
for Dr. Cindy Daly

Beauty is more than skin deep
Tell that to the Mona Lisa.

My face never launched
a single rowboat,
stopped a train
or sped up a Nascar race
but it was mine
and I loved its hawk-like lines.

Once, I preened
       in front of windows
admired
         my reflection
in puddles and shiny pot-lids

and now—

thanks to my dear surgeon
who restored my shattered nose

I will resume my rituals.

TESTS OF THE HEART

Family Tree

Great grandfather Charles
opened the fridge for a beer
and lay in a cooler hours later.
Grandpa Dick keeled over a bleacher
in Montreal's baseball stadium.

Uncle Bob was bagged on a mountain-side
and brother Gary, who dodged Vietnam
froze as he shoveled snow.

Today, the branched family blossoms
on blood pressure pills
and enough warfarin to poison
a shipload of rats.

Panting along trails and treadmills
eyes glued to meters,
they pedal while the timekeeper
housed in their hearts
waits in his plush purple chambers.

4 a.m.

I reach for my ipad
music to lull me
to sleep

A message beeps then flashes:

RENÉ— HEART ATTACK

My limbs lurch
My vision blurs
I struggle for breath

*NO NO NO, not my son
Not him not him not him*

My howls wake my husband;
he reads the rest of the text—

René collapsed playing hockey,
main arteries blocked,
stents being put in …

My love, my darling child,
hope rips me open like birth—

I pray the tunnel-shaped stents
will channel
his life-blood home

Vigil

In the glass-fronted
room to our left
a woman with violet skin
lies stiff as a dried petal.

In the room to our right—
two girls in saffron saris
hold hands, weeping
over a draped figure.

Brushing back my own tears,
I wonder how many
have risen from your bed,
their ghosts unfolding
like white sheets stacked
in the cupboard beside you.

René

I chose your name
because it means
rebirth,
renaissance, and the first
April snowdrops.

Your nickname arrived years later
when a perky *wren*
laid her eggs
in the hollowed gourd-house
I bought for your 40th birthday.

Proud appellation of dukes, bishops, judges,
famous soldiers and sages, I recall
you once said in high school:
Philosophy (unlike math or science)
is an easy credit. To pass the test
all I must do is prove
a line from René Descartes:
I think, therefore I am.

No, my son, proof isn't that easy.
I squeeze back tears at your bedside
as your newly-mended heart flutters.
You have to keep breathing,
you have to keep waking,
you need to start drinking and eating
and walking and laughing and crying.

Do anything
except dying.

Looking at Old Postcards

You are four,
traveling across Europe with your
brother and newly divorced dad
who has custody.

Two weeks after your flight,
postcards land in my mailbox.

Your father has set down your words:
I love you, mom. I miss you.

My eyes caress your signature—

The wobbly colt legs of the R
the backwards tines of the E
the left-leaning capital N
and the final flipped È,
its accent tipped towards
the ground instead of the sky.

Had this been our trip
I'd have given up the sight
of the Eiffel Tower at sunset,
the grand gardens of Versailles,
the Trevi Fountains flanked
by Tritons and seahorses,
and all those Venetian gondolas
gliding across your cards
to hold you in my arms.

Growing Up

At six you told me your dream—

*When I grow up
I will have a farm with three horses,
red, black and gold. There will be
a chicken house with twenty-five chicks
and a pond for my fish and ducks.*

*One day, in the middle of winter
a big storm will come.
I'll light a fire in my stove
and cook a delicious dinner.
When it's ready I will hear
a knock on my door and it will be
my mother come back to live with me.*

    ***

René, if I could greet you in the past
I'd light birch logs in the fireplace.
Your favorite dinner would steam on the stove.
No snow would ever storm your house
in spring, summer or fall.
Your fish would ripple sunbeams on the pond;
we'd gather the hens' eggs together.
Your palominos would graze
in the greenest of meadows.

On the farm where we'd live
I would finally grow up,
love you more than my dreams for myself,
and stay with you forever.

What hurts most

Your little daughter
who wrote your name
in the dark with sparklers
lit from a bonfire,

your "little goose"
who paddled with you
on Pine Lake and decorated
your hair with feathers,

your princess who put on fashion shows,
beaded a necklace for you,
and called you her Very Best Friend,

your Gumby girl who did back flips
and wound her arms round your neck
as you watched *Dumb and Dumber* together,

your girl now confronted
with needles and noisy monitors,
metal trees hung with vines
snaking into your nightgown,
the stranger who sucks phials of blood
from the port taped to your wrist,

your girl you love more than your life
freezes against the wall—

Standing Guard

By his father's hospital bed
my grandson, age fourteen, stands.

Fists balled, teeth clenched,
he's   *taking it*
              taking it

one ragged breath at a time
while his father struggles for air

Afraid to cry   *Dad I love you*
              please fight for life

with memories of
rough-housing and male taunts
… words he wants to forget—

*Dad, you've got a gut
bigger than Jabba the Hutt.*

*Dad don't be a wuss
go punch out our beach-hogging neighbour.*

Ethan's nails score
sliver moons in his palms,
brown eyes blacken to midnight

taking it
    taking it

one hard blow at a time—

his father in a gown
name braceleting his wrist

he who reeled in
a king-sized Pine-Lake pike

his dad hooked up to IV now

taking it   without tears
braving it all   like a man.

Ode to an IV Tree

Despite leafless limbs,
rootless metal trunk
no woodpecker tap-holes
where chickadees might take shelter
from winter's snowy wings,

despite your acorn-dearth,
green needles to stitch the sky,
or the maple keys children stick
on their noses, pretending
they can fly,

despite the absence of canopy,
ring-count of your years,
and the afterlife of choice wood
singing from a violin
or fashioning a table and chairs,
you too are bountiful.

Your saline sap suspended
in clear plastic sacs, drips
from your truncated boughs,
trickles into my son's blue veins.

Safeguarding him
from the blight that might come
after heart surgery, you nourish him
till he's strong enough
to sip apple juice and reach out
to the taste of cherries
brightening the bowl by his bed.

Because

you resumed breathing, my son
my lungs no longer ache.

Because your blue lips turned pink,
I bloom with your gift shop roses.

Because you opened your eyes,
I do not fear sunset seeping
through cracked blinds.

Because you swallowed
a spoonful of soup,
I can break my fast.

Because your heart beats in rhythm,
mine floats up to the ceiling
and nuzzles
your get-well balloons.

Umbilical

Patches of glue
from the electrodes
stick to your chest and belly
—a second grey skin
that won't dissolve in the shower
or peel off with alcohol.
Lighter fluid would do it,
you say with a little black laugh.

I rub each patch
with my fingertips
till the film beads into balls
I roll onto a wash cloth,
then gently
       caress the coating
            that clings
to the spot
       near your navel.

Tips

There are tears on the tips of twigs,
tears in the creases of leaves,
and diamonds on spider webs.

It's been raining for weeks, I tell myself
as if that could explain
the tears that still puddle my pillow,
salting the long strands of my hair,
the tiny tears
that splash my dinner plate
and tip the asparagus wands,
the sudden drops I can't stanch
remembering you almost died.

Angels

after electronic sculptures by OGE Group, Israel

Three pairs of wired wings,
each with a heart at its centre, cast
coloured shadows in the courtyard.

As passersby pose for glowing
selfies in front of them,
I laud your angels—

the teammate who called 911,
the paramedics who zapped
your quivering core,
your nurse-practitioner sister
who cheered your first new breaths,
your brother who helped you take heart
by streaming a hockey game
into your hospital room,
and the surgeon who later said,
"You lucky dog, you've been saved."

Blessed be those guardians,
who wrapped their wings around you
and delivered you back to me,
whole,
safely reborn René.

Helium

I recall you at five
with your helium balloon—
stars sparkling its skin,
and a bunch of blue and red streamers
tied to its stem like a kite's tail.

You loved that balloon-brother,
talked to it as a friend,
ran with gazelle grace across the park
towing it after you.

Too young to know that helium
is lighter than air,
you let go of the string.

As it lifted
above treetops and roofs
out of your tiptoed reach,
instead of crying and begging me
to buy you another,
you clapped your hands and shouted,
have fun in the sky!

Tests of the Heart

Yesterday a friend
who was reading "Lord of the Rings"
asked if I knew anyone like Frodo,
good-hearted and worthy enough
to carry the ring to Mordor.

I recalled the test, jagged
with peaks and valleys
of your heart's ragged rhythm,
the Echo that sounded
its chambers and caves,
the dye that blued the blockade
where white blood cells
converged like Orcs on the wound
after the plaque broke away.

I considered your disposition as sunny
as a six-foot hobbit who preferred
cottage-life on a backroad,
fishing, hiking and skiing
to the hunt for a glint of gold.
I gave you points for the time
your clench-fisted neighbor complained
when your kids trespassed on his beach,
your peace-offering—
a bottle of amber maple syrup
and access to your red canoe.

Yes, I traced the scars on your vessels
from your motherless childhood
and the father who later deserted you.
I treasured the sprouts
that inched from our lives
after you welcomed us back.

I noted the far-away look,
flash of pain in your eyes
when blood tests proved
you were marked for
a journey you could never refuse.

Yes, I knew you'd carry
your own ring of temptation
to bitterness, anger and darkness
as close to the fire as you could.
You'd travel with hard-won grace,
your circle of comrades
and your older brother, standing by you,
stalwart as Samwise.

Yes, I answered the question sadly yet proudly:
My good-hearted son, René.

Thanksgiving

Because you were shocked back to life
after your heart stopped, René,
every day is Thanksgiving.

Instead of replaying your birth
when you pushed through my portal
coated in waxy snowflakes
and waving your tiny clenched fists,

in lieu of counting
fingers and toes, tracing
your quarter-moon brows,
little conch ears and the bridge
of your perfect nose, I marvel
at your middle-aged fingers
cupped around a latté
and give thanks
for your palms nesting
your daughter's hand, and read
the lines on your forehead
comforting as a letter home.

Waiting on a pre-Cambrian boulder
beached near your brother's cottage,
I brim with the sight of you
in your red canoe,
baseball cap and blue shorts,
      paddling the treacherous bay
    closer
        and closer to us.

THE STORIES THAT WRITE US

DNA

The stories that write us
can't be told
on parchment, birch-bark, linen or paper.
They need no quills, charcoal or pens
nor traveling
tongues of storytellers.

The tales that tell us
stretch their beginnings
on our rose petal skin
and lengthening limbs.
They flesh out their plots
in our bloodstreams and bones
as we become subjects and objects
in a relentless saga.

Today, explorers in lab coats dream
of sweetening our chronicles
by sealing the mouths of flawed cells
and revising our roster of genes.
To prolong our primes
and edit imperfect endings,
they aim to alter our alphabets.

Sapphira's Story
adapted from the bible, Acts 5

My husband, Ananias and I
sold a tract of *our* land
and gave the money to the Apostle
to dole out to the poor.
The hitch was, being a farmer's wife
who'd milked many a cow,
I skimmed some off the top
instead of giving the whole amount
like I bragged to Peter.

Well, being an accountant,
God audited my lie.
His brimstone breath melted me
into a clay-coloured lump
he shaped as he pleased.

My ghost has moved on.
I hitchhiked through
the centuries into the nunnery
of Hildegard and learned
to read and write.
I picketed with the suffragettes
and chained myself to the White House fence.
In 2001, I went to Toronto,
got a law degree.

Now that I, Sapphira, B.A., LL.D
dare speak officially, I propose
we put God on trial
for unjust behavior and inhumanity.

As for myself, the life I lost
can never be replaced.
But the very least God owes me
for my charity is a tax credit
or a lump sum settlement
payable to my descendants—
back-dated to 25 A.D.

Dinah Nuthead*
      Saint Mary's Historic City, Maryland, 1660

You leering old lawyer!

How easy to guess your thoughts
when I grip the press's long black handle
we call *the devil's tail.*

My bosom bouncing and heaving
as I push and pull
        the lever
                that lowers
the platen on to the press board
after the letters are inked,
I wager you wish
you were Old Nick himself unlacing
my bodice while I pump
his tool that never tires,
unlike your own member.

Later, when you doze
like a dog by the hearth waiting
for your contracts to dry
I stroke a *G* and a *D*, and pray
you never discover
I'd give a slice of my soul
to learn the couplings of letters
that can spell sun moon and stars
the secrets of warts and wings,
fly me past drudgery.

I can't stop playing
with the alphabet-blocks
lined up in the devil's hell-box
though I'm scared
by the *i*'s severed head,
the teeth of the *E*
and the *Y* that insists on asking:

Why must a woman
who teaches herself to read
be suspected of witchery?

Origami
    for André

My son at fifty tells me:

When I was a little boy
I loved to watch Grandpa
reading the newspaper—

He'd fold each section in halves
        quarters
                eighths,
flattening each perfect crease.

Tipping the news side to side,
flipping it over
            and over,
  opening   closing
                    triangles,
        intricate panels and flaps
like the wings
      of an elaborate origami,
he'd read to me about
animals that predict earthquakes,
Space Mountain opening at Disneyland,
the film release of "Jaws"
before he'd lift and scan
the fins of the stock market page.

Listening,
I, who can only recall
my father disappearing
   behind a centrefold
spread to escape me,
now marvel at my son
       delicately
unfolding
          his grandfather's shapes and sides
with the love of a *kami* master.

The Many Holes in a Snowflake
for André

There are nostrils
mouths and ear-holes,
pinpricks and peepholes,
O's that lead to China
the dykes of Holland
and the levees in New Orleans.

There are loopholes like alibis,
wounds like bullet holes
or the ones in Leonard Cohen's line,
"He gave her a flake of his life."

And when the snow sifts down today,
I imagine a math wizard
adding up centuries of tiny holes
as he tries to calculate
how many zeroes
there are in infinity.

So many snowflakes—
riddled with shining spaces
lovely because of their O's
and because they fall
as we also fall
from grace
and from God—
our souls holy, like snowflakes.

A year after your passing, mom

The loon at sunset
   carries
        her chicks
     on her buoyant back
through Georgian Bay

Undaunted
     by white-plumed waves
            flying at her
       from the wakes
         of ships and sea-doos
she bobs
     between sharp boulders
and the tossing
       shadow of an osprey

As the light ripples
    rose and orange
and she nears
      her woven nest
lined with moss and down

I still pine for an impossible refuge

Sparrow

Non, rien de rien.
Non, Je ne regrette rien
sings sparrow Edith Piaf
on the branches of her life

Non, Je ne regrette rien, I sing back to her
when my love and I lie close
as winter foxes curled up in a cave

No, I'm not sorry, the child I once was
belts out at my father
I hate you
then slams herself in a closet

No, I regret nothing, I smile
after birth pangs split
me open and I stroke
my blood-stained firstborn

No, I'd do it again, I cry
even after two divorces.
No no no, I refuse to regret my sins
contained in the confessional:
the hearts I ripped like tissue paper,
the fledgling I chose
to have sucked from my womb,
the third child I gave life to
and learned to love
more than myself

Non, rien de rien, I sing
to my dog who digs up my garden,
to the ice-pick stars,
the salt-rivers on Mars,
the pocked face of the moon
and the cosmic dust I'll become

No, I regret nothing, I hope
I'll shout into the chasm of nothing
that will silence
my heartbeat and tongue that dares
to affirm with that little black sparrow,
Non, Je ne regrette rien.

Brimming

for my son, James

You give me a birthday bouquet—
incandescent sunflowers.

The stems could topple my vase
but I don't saw them shorter
because (though my spine is shrinking)
I try to stand tall and straight.

I'm glad you bring me these "goldies"
studded with rings of brown seeds
instead of ghostly white lilies
or a potted Organ Pipe cactus
that reminds me of funeral dirges
pumped out on a parish church organ.

Wishing my own harvest could be
     whorls
of wind-stormed petals—
I could inch up in spring
like the withered Lord of Autumn,
reborn from a sunflower seed,

I blow out my birthday candles
and turn my face,
        brimming,
               towards you.

An Old Yarn

The stork carries a blanket in her beak—
a new baby she will leave
on a doorstep.
             That's how you came
into the world, grandma told me.
She flew millions of miles, braving
mountains, oceans and windstorms,
careful never to drop you.

Rewinding my grandmother's yarn—

Careful never to drop me,
that stork will carry
my old woman-soul in her warm blanket.
She'll fly me beyond
all doorsteps and roofs
through cosmic storms and galaxies
to bring me home.

END NOTES

p. 3: Ozymandias: a sonnet written by Percy Bysshe Shelley.

p. 10: Saul, why are you persecuting me? Recorded in the Acts of the Apostles, The Conversion of St. Paul.

p. 12: Huberdeau: a town in the Laurentian Mountains, Quebec.

p. 13: Caribou: a popular French-Canadian wine.

p. 14: Maniple: a priestly garment consisting of a strip of material hanging from the left arm.

p. 14: Paten: a plate with a handle.

p. 15: Catholic nunneries usually requested a dowry in exchange for accepting the daughters. For poor families with many children this could be a small amount unlike a real marriage dowry with the added benefit of reaping an eternal reward.

p. 24: Anne Savage belonged to Montreal's Beaver Hall Group of Canadian painters (1910) notable because it included women artists.

p. 25: Sortilege: a mixture of whisky and maple syrup.

DISCLAIMER: TO STAY AFLOAT
All the Niagara Falls poems in this section are works of fiction loosely based on the lives of their characters.

p. 31: On Oct. 24, 1901, Annie Edson Taylor, accompanied by her cat, became the first person and the first woman to go over Horseshoe Falls in a barrel.

p. 34: Bobby Leach, a British stuntman, was the first man to make a successful trip over Niagara Falls in a steel barrel on July 25, 1911. The words in italics are his.

p. 36: Charles G. Stephens (1862-1920) was the first of the Niagara Falls stuntmen to lose his life. His arm (the only part of him that was ever found) was buried in Floaters' Corner, a section of Drummond Hill cemetery in Niagara Falls, the resting place for the unidentified remains of victims of the Falls.

p. 38: On July 4, 1930, George Stathakis and his pet turtle, Sonny rode over Horseshoe Falls in a barrel hoping that the revenue generated from the stunt could be used to publish his book on metaphysical experiences. Only the turtle survived.

p. 40: Nathan Boya, AKA, William Fitzgerald, was the first African-American to go over Niagara Falls on July 15, 1961 and the first person to be arrested and fined for not obtaining a permit for his stunt. There is much speculation about his guarded life, but he did appear as a contestant on T.V. shows.
—adapted from Wiki and other internet sources

All quotes are from T.S. Eliot, "The Love Song of J. Alfred Prufrock." except the last one, which is from Nathan Boya.

p. 42: Karel Soucek was born in Czechoslovakia in 1947 and lived in Hamilton, Ontario. He conquered Niagara Falls in a barrel on July 2, 1984 and died in 1989 in the Houston Astrodome.

p. 44: Jesse W. Sharp, a twenty-eight-year-old bachelor from Ocoee, Tennessee, lost his life on June 5, 1990 in an attempt to project himself in a kayak over Horseshoe Falls.

p. 46: On June 19, 1995, Lori Martin accompanied Steve Trotter on his second successful trip over Horseshoe Falls. Trotter was fined and spent two weeks in jail. In 1997, Lori Martin broke a vertebra in her neck after accompanying him on a "Tarzan Swing" off Golden Gate Bridge in San Francisco—adapted from Wiki and other sources.

p. 58: *Square eggs*: powdered eggs with milk and cheese baked in a square pan.

p. 58: *Shit on a shingle:* creamed beef chips on toast.

p. 69: Missing noses and other bodily parts were a popular theme in the 1800's, eg, Nikolai Gogol's short story, *The Nose*.

p. 102: Dinah Nuthead helped her husband run a printing press in St. Mary's Historic City, Maryland circa 1660. Though she probably knew the letters of the alphabet, she couldn't read or write. At that time, only judges, lawyers and clergymen were literate.

p. 106: *Famous Blue Raincoat,* a song by Leonard Cohen.

p. 108: *Rien de Rien* (no, nothing of nothing) A French song composed by Charles Dumont with lyrics by Michel Vaucaire.

ACKNOWLEDGEMENTS

The following poems or versions have been published in—

In Lieu of an Ode won an Honourable Mention award in *The Epic Proportions* contest and was published in a chapbook by the Ontario Poetry Society, 2017.

Candles for Gary was awarded Second Place in the poetry competition, and The Blue Sleigh was a Judge's Choice for publication in the 32nd volume of *The Banister*, 2017 (Canadian Authors Association, Niagara branch)

Benediction appeared in E-Zine *Big Pond Rumours*, Feb. 2018.

Daring Niagara, Keeping Your Word, and Le Calvaire D'Huberdeau, appeared in online *Morel Magazine*, Nov. 2016.

The Hand, Watching a Film Clip and Lady Niagara Falls were all published in *The Saving Banister*, volume 31, 2016, (Canadian Authors Association, Niagara Branch)

The Orange Revenge: *Arbolealis Anthology,* The Ontario Poetry Society, 2016.

The Man Who Slept Beside Torpedoes (entire suite): 2nd prize, *GritLIT competition*, 2014.

Ode to an IV Tree was published in the League of Canadian Poets *Heartwood Anthology.*

Dinah Nuthead: CWS/cf (*Canadian Woman Studies*) 2016

DNA: was published in *Lummox Anthology* 6, USA

The Many Holes in a Snowflake: *From O to Snow Anthology*, Hidden Brook Press, 2010.

A year after your passing, Mom: *Drafts,* 2014.

Sparrow was published in Art Rewired, Vol. 1, No. 3 of *The Artis* Magazine.

A SPECIAL THANK YOU TO:

James Dewar, my publisher/editor for his faith in me and the ten wonderful years of Hot Sauced Words challenges which inspired several of these poems.

Sue Reynolds, for the wonderfully reflective cover image.

Chris Pannell and Kate Rogers for tough honest critiques.

Katie Marshall-Flaherty for editing and her Still Point Workshops that sparked many poems.

John B. Lee and poet/musician Dr. Tom Gannon Hamilton who helped my words to sing.

Rosemary Clewes, Mary Baxter, Terry Burns, James Comeaux, Ann Carson, Deborah Panko, Richard Reinert for much appreciated suggestions.

Donna Langevin

Donna Langevin, a retired teacher and mother of three sons, wears a triple hat. Poet and playwright, co-author of four ESL books, she is a long-time resident of Toronto. Her latest poetry collections include *The Laundress of Time*, Aeolus House 2015, *In the Café du Monde*, Hidden Brook Press 2008 and two chapbooks with Lyricalmyrical Press. She won first prize in the TOPS Contest 2008 and also in the Cyclamens and Swords contest 2009. She was short-listed for the *Descant* 2010 Winston Collins prize and was awarded second prize in the GritLIT Poetry Competition 2014 and second prize in The Banister Anthology competition 2017.

About Donna's plays: *The Man with a Butterfly Hat* was produced at the Toronto Alumnae Theatre New Ideas Festival, 2012. *Welcome to Nuit Blanche* was produced at the Ryerson 50+ Festival, 2014. *The Dinner*, published by Morel magazine, won first prize for script in the one act play contest for the 2014 Eden Mills Writers' Festival as did *Bargains in the New World* in 2015. *If Socrates Were in My Shoes* was produced at Alumnae Theatre NIF, 2018.